I0504940

# The Door to Success in Hong Kong
*10 Practical Tips for Starting and Running Businesses*

by Eunice Chu

# CONTENTS

# PREFACE

Hong Kong ranked as the world's number one freest economy for the 25<sup>th</sup> successive year, beginning in 1995, beating out Singapore, which landed at second place. Hong Kong is the gateway to the 1.4 billion people that make up the Chinese market. No matter what kind of passport one holds, everyone is welcome to set up a business in Hong Kong without any restrictions.

Hong Kong is the international financial center, and its capital market ranked number one in the IPO market worldwide from 2009 to 2011 as well as in 2015, 2016, and 2018. It offers excellent Internet banking services to both corporate and small and medium enterprises. It adopts a common law system and has clear and well-defined regulations. With its proximity to the Asia Pacific region, it is also the ideal place for setting up regional headquarters.

In this city, there is no minimum capital requirement, no sales tax, no VAT, no capital gains taxes, and no requirements for local directors or shareholders. A limited company can be set up in one working day with minimal costs, and it can also be de-registered easily. The tax rate for profits is as low as 8.25%, with a 16.5% maximum.

Hong Kong is a very exciting place for startups that want to test out their ideas, entrepreneurs that aim to expand their businesses in Asia, and large corporations that want to tap into the increasing purchasing power of the huge market in China.

With over 20 years of experience helping large and small businesses to establish and expand their businesses in Hong Kong, I have accumulated profound knowledge and a great understanding of the difficulties and concerns that most entrepreneurs face when they start and develop their business. These ten practical tips for doing great business in Hong Kong can not only serve as a roadmap for your business but also give you more confidence as you develop your entrepreneurship.

"Dream big, work hard, stay focused and surround yourself with good people."
– LiveLifeHappy.com

Good luck pursuing your dream!

## ABOUT THE AUTHOR

Eunice Chu is a Certified Public Accountant (CPA) in Hong Kong. Trained in one of the Big 4 international accounting firms, she has solid business and technical knowledge. Eunice also gained extensive senior finance management experience while working as the regional finance director of a U.S.-listed company and a Fortune 500 multinational corporation.

Over the years, Eunice has helped numerous businesses start up, relocate, and settle in Hong Kong. From her vast experience of working with both small and medium-sized entities, Eunice has developed a thorough understanding of the needs and challenges entrepreneurs face when they build their business in Hong Kong.

Eunice speaks to corporations, associations, forums, and training events; conducts research projects; and contributes to articles and media commentaries.

Apart from work, Eunice loves skiing and dancing.

Connect with Eunice at: eunicechuchu@gmail.com

Facebook: Eunice Chu Chu – Accounting

LinkedIn: Eunice Chu

Chapter 1 : 10 Steps to Setting Up a Limited Company in Hong Kong

**W**hen a person carries on a business or trade in Hong Kong, he or she has to set up a company in accordance with the Hong Kong Companies Ordinance (Chapter 622). There are no restrictions on who can set up businesses in Hong Kong. In other words, you can set up a Hong Kong company even if you don't have a Hong Kong identity card, you don't live in Hong Kong, or you don't even plan to visit Hong Kong at all. Below, I will outline the 10 steps you should follow to set up your company:

### 1. Determine the type of company.

Before you begin setting up your business, you will need to explore if you want to set up a sole proprietorship, partnership, or limited company.

   a) Sole proprietorship

     In what circumstances should you choose sole

proprietorship? 1) If you are a Hong Kong identity card holder, 2) you just want to test your business idea, or 3) the business risk is low. If any of these fit your situation, then you can consider setting up a sole proprietorship. The advantage of a sole proprietorship is that the setup and closing procedures are simple, and the setup and running costs are low. However, the disadvantage of a sole proprietorship is unlimited liability. When the sole proprietorship becomes insolvent, the sole proprietor has to settle the debts of the sole proprietorship with his or her own personal assets. The sole proprietorship offers the owner little protection from business risks.

b) Partnerships
   According to the Hong Kong Companies Ordinance, a partnership can be owned by more than one person but not more than 20 persons. Similar to the sole proprietorship, the advantages of a partnership are simple setup and closing procedures and low setup and running costs. In the same way, the disadvantage of a partnership is unlimited liability. When the partnership becomes insolvent, the partners of the partnership have to settle the debts of the partnership with their own personal assets.

Normally I would not suggest business owners setting up a partnership because the risk is high.

Any one partner can commit the partnership to any contracts, which will then become legally binding to all partners. Additionally, partners are jointly and severally liable for their partners, which means that any one partner may be held responsible for losses of the whole business and not limited to his or her actual share of the losses.

If one of the partners enters into a commercially disadvantageous business contract, such as committing the partnership to delivering goods or services on an unrealistic schedule or otherwise needing to pay huge compensation to the customer, all the partners would be legally bound to share and pay the huge compensation. If the other partners do not have sufficient personal assets, the one who has sufficient personal assets needs to be responsible for the whole loss of the partnership and is not just limited to his or her share of the loss. In my personal opinion, the business risk of a partnership is even higher than that of the sole proprietorship.

c) Limited company

This is the most common and formal form of business establishment. Although the running costs are higher, a limited company offers maximum protection to its investors, who are re-

ferred to as "members" or "shareholders." When the limited company becomes insolvent and unable to pay its debts, the shareholders are not obliged to settle the debts with their own personal assets. The limited company is a legal entity that is independent from its owners.

A limited company can be owned by one investor or a maximum of 50 investors, according to the Hong Kong Companies Ordinance (Chapter 622).

## 2. Determine the company's name.
If you are setting up a sole proprietorship or partnership, there is no restriction on the name of the sole proprietorship or partnership.

However, for a limited company you will need to perform a name search exercise at the website of the Companies Registry to confirm no one is currently using that name before the name can be used. The name search can be done by using the link below:

https://www.icris.cr.gov.hk/csci/

If someone is already using the name of the limited

company you have chosen, you can vary the name by adding words, such as "international," "global," "enterprise," "Asia," etc. to differentiate the existing companies from the one you are going to set up.

### 3. Describe the nature of the business in one sentence

To apply for a business registration license, you need to describe the nature of the business in one sentence; this will be shown on the business license. For example, the company's description can be "provide business consulting services," "provide digital marketing services," "online distribution of consumer products," etc.

In Hong Kong, the business nature stipulated on the business license would not restrict your subsequent business activities. For example, if your business nature is online distribution of consumer products but you subsequently would like to provide services to advise people how to run an online shop, you can do so without the need to reapply for a new business license with the government.

### 4. Define the shareholding

If you are setting up a sole proprietorship, then you will be the owner of the company.

If you are setting up a partnership, then you and your partners will be the owners of the partnership. You need to define the percentage of ownership.

When you set up a limited company, you need to

determine the shareholdings. It can be in any combination, such as 50% vs. 50%, 90% vs. 10%, etc.

The following documents are required:

a)   Identity proof: This can be a copy of a Hong Kong identity card or a passport from any country. A foreigner with or without a Hong Kong identity card is also allowed to become one of the shareholders of a Hong Kong limited company. However, to become a sole proprietor in a sole proprietorship or a partner in a partnership, he or she needs to hold a valid Hong Kong identity card or appoint a representative who holds a Hong Kong identity card to act on his or her behalf.

b)   Residential proof: Residential proof can be a utility bill issued to the person's name within three months. The residential address can be one located in or outside Hong Kong. However, it should be an address that the sole proprietor, partner, shareholder, or director can receive correspondence at.

**5. Directors**

Only limited companies have directors, who are responsible for managing and running the companies. They can be one of the shareholders or they can be employees of the company. Each limited company needs to have at least one director. It can have more than one to form the board of directors.

Directors have full power over the companies. They

can direct the day-to-day operations and commit the companies to any contracts. They also have full responsibility for the actions of the companies.

To become the director of a limited company, the following documents are required:
(A) a copy of the Hong Kong identity card or passport and
(B) the address proof (a utility bill issued to the name of the director within three months).

### 6. Company secretary

A limited company must have a company secretary. When a person is a shareholder and director at the same time, he or she cannot act as the company secretary. Because of this, many small and medium enterprises (SMEs) usually outsource the role of the company secretary to the "Trust and Company Secretary Providers" (TCSP), which needs to obtain a license from the Companies Registry.

It is advised that you request to inspect their TCSP license before you commit to employing a company to act as your company secretary.

A company secretary has no power over the company. He or she cannot commit the company to any contract. His or her role is simply to prepare documents for the company to comply with the Hong Kong Companies Ordinance (Chapter 622). Given the company secretary has no power over the company, it is suggested that SMEs outsource this role to a professional TCSP to ensure proper regulatory compliance.

## 7. Registered address

All kinds of companies, including sole proprietorships, partnerships, and limited companies, are required to have a registered address in Hong Kong. This serves as a correspondence address with the Hong Kong government. The registered address can be the same or different from the operation address. It can be a residential building as well. Hence, some companies will use the residential address of one of the directors or shareholders as the registered address.

However, it is recommended that businesses use the addresses of the company secretary as the registered address since company secretaries are well trained to handle documents from the government, and they can advise you on how to handle these properly and efficiently. If government correspondence is mailed to the residential address of one of the directors or shareholders, they may fail to understand the urgency or to respond appropriately. Moreover, if they move and fail to inform the government, there would be a breakdown of communication between the government and the company, which would likely result in late charges and penalties.

## 8. Subsequent changes in the company structure

When there is a subsequent change of the sole proprietor in the sole proprietorship, it is considered that the original sole proprietorship is dissolved and replaced by a new sole proprietorship. The same applies to a partnership.

For a limited company, a director can resign and be replaced by a new director. The shares of one shareholder can also be transferred to a new shareholder. Similarly, new shareholders can be admitted. New shares can be issued to the existing or new shareholders. All of these changes can be affected through preparing documents and filing them with the Companies Registry. You can consult your company secretary to do this, or you can visit the website of the Companies Registry to download the forms.

https://www.cr.gov.hk/en/home/index.htm

## 9. Timing
When all of the documents are ready and you work through the authorized Trust and Company Secretary Providers, a sole proprietorship, partnership, or limited company can be set up in only one working day. However, to allow for a buffer, you should allow three working days to be safe.

## 10. Set up documents issued by the government
When a sole proprietorship or partnership is properly set up, only a business license will be issued by the Hong Kong government as the official setup document.

When a limited company is properly set up, you

should get the following documents:

a) Certificate of incorporation

b) Business registration license

c) A full company kit, sometimes referred to as a green box, which consists of the following:
- a booklet of share certificates
- a register for recording the directors, shareholders, minutes, and charges
- a round, pre-inked stamp
- an authorized signature pre-inked stamp
- a metal seal to be used in signing formal contracts

If you have any further questions, please feel free to email me at eunicechuchu@gmail.com.

# CHAPTER 2: OPENING A BANK ACCOUNT

Once your company has been set up, the next step will be opening a bank account. This is no longer a simple procedure.

As a result of the U.S. legislation entitled "Foreign Account Tax Compliance Act" (FATCA) and "Anti-Money Laundering/Combating the Financing of Terrorism" (AMT-CTF), the compliance burden of financial institutions has greatly increased. Hence, all banks have to perform "Know Your Customers"' (KYC) and "Customer Due Diligence" (CDD) exercises before they can accept a new customer.

As limited companies are the most common form of business establishment, the procedures discussed below relate to limited companies.

All shareholders and directors need to be physically present in the interview with the bank officers during the bank account opening process.

To succeed in opening a bank account with a traditional bank, you need to show the following during the interview with the bank officers:
1. You know your business well.
2. You have the ability and experience to lead

a sustainable business.
3. You are well educated and possess relevant education and experience in the field.
4. Ideally, the business already has some trading records.
5. The products or services you are providing are not disposed to money laundering.
6. You do not trade in any countries or deal with any organizations that are blacklisted by the United Nations.

The documents required to open a bank account include, but are not limited to, the following:
1. Setup documents of your company: certificate of incorporation, business registration license, NNC1 form that shows the details of the directors and shareholders
2. Copies of the Hong Kong identity cards or passports of all directors and shareholders
3. Copies of the address proofs (utilities bills or bank statements issued within three months) for all directors and shareholders
4. Business plan: A brief summary of your company's business model. I suggest you download your website, which should describe the products the company sells or services it provides. Alternatively, you can simply fill in our template that is included at the end of this chapter as a starting point for constructing your simple business plan for the purpose of opening a bank account.

5. An organization chart to show the share-holding structure of the company
6. A letter issued by the certified public accountant to confirm the particulars of the company are correct
7. A list of customers
8. Sales invoices issued or suppliers' invoices received so far
9. Other bank statements of the company, if any
10. Financial forecast for the next three years (you can seek help from your accountant)
11. Personal bank statements of the directors or shareholders, if available

## The procedure used to set up a bank account

1. Call the SME business centers of the bank and make a reservation.
2. All the directors and shareholders have to be physically present in the meeting to be interviewed by the bank officer.
3. Bring all documents to the bank officers at the meeting.
4. Get the business card of the bank officer you meet with in the meeting so that you can send documents to him or her later on if they require further information.

## Online banking and a corporate credit card or debit card

Online banking and debit cards should be applied when the corporate bank account is first set up.

Once the bank account is ready, you can operate the bank account remotely via internet banking.

Regarding corporate credit cards, banks are reluctant to grant credit cards until the company has a history with them. I suggest using a designated personal credit card for business purposes and letting the company settle that designated personal credit card as if it were the corporate credit card.

## Question that will be asked

To better prepare yourself for the interview with the bank officers, these are some of the typical questions:

1. What is the business model?
2. Briefly explain the target customers; the operating flow from sourcing, promotion, delivery of products or services; billing of customers; and collection of money.
3. What are the products or services your company is offering? Describe the unique features of the products or services your company is offering and how customers are identifying with your product or service.
4. Is any additional staffing needed? If yes, what is your recruitment plan?
5. What is the expected revenue in the first three years?
6. What are the number of receipts and payments per month?
7. What are the expected amounts per transaction? For example, $100,000 to

$500,000 or $1 million to $5 million?

8. Are any cross-border receipts or payments expected? If yes, from which countries to which countries? And what would be the expected amounts?

9. Why do you need a Hong Kong bank account if all the directors or staff are located outside Hong Kong?

10. Are there any planned major assets acquisitions, such as real estate?

11. What is the company's operating address (not registered address)? It can be in a co-working location, and it can be located outside Hong Kong.

## Annual customer due diligence (CDD) performed by banks

According to the regulatory requirements, banks have to perform annual CDD on selected bank accounts. If you are among the selected samples, give this situation top priority and care. You should ensure proper documents are prepared and uploaded to the portal in a timely manner. If the bank officers request phone interviews with the directors of the company, you should accommodate them as much as possible.

During the phone interview, the interviewees should show full knowledge of the company's operations, including the number of receipt transactions and payment transactions per month, the estimated range of size of each receipt or payments, the number of customers and suppliers, the business operation model, and more.

Failing to properly handle the CDD could result in the bank account being frozen and eventually closed. You should also seek help from those local company secretaries who are experienced in handling CDD.

### Do you need a traditional bank account?

Some companies, especially startups, experience difficulties in setting up bank accounts with traditional banks because they lack historical trading records. I have two suggestions:

### 1. Consider a Neat Account

Neat is a fintech company located in Hong Kong. They maintain a bank account with Standard Chartered Bank and then subdivide its bank accounts and distribute them to SMEs. The money is sitting in Standard Chartered Bank but on the Neat platform.

The advantage of a Neat account is that it is easier to set up. Directors and shareholders do not need to be physically present in Hong Kong to meet with the bank officers. You can upload the documents online. It is quicker to set up the bank account (3 to 7 working days), but the downside is that they are more expensive since they charge a service fee for each transaction.

Some people still do not have full faith in the Neat platform. They use it as receipt and payment medium but not as an account for holding their cash. When their balances begin to accumulate, they transfer that amount to their personal bank accounts, which are maintained by traditional banks.

## 2. Use PayPal, Visa, Mastercard, Western Union, PayMe, or Alipay

If you are involved in a retail business and selling to overseas consumers, you may consider accepting international payments from other means, such as PayPal, Visa, Mastercard, or Western Union. If you are selling to consumers locally in Hong Kong, you may consider PayMe, Alipay (Hong Kong payment platform), Octopus, Tap&Go, etc.

All of these online payment platforms can then be linked back either to a traditional corporate bank account or a personal bank account specially designated for the use of the business.

To use a personal bank account specifically designated for business purposes is not ideal. However, this may provide an interim solution for many small startup business owners.

If you require further assistance, please feel free to contact me at eunicechuchu@gmail.com.

## Appendix

### Business Plan

| | |
|---|---|
| Company name: | ■ Company name |
| Business nature: | ■ Trading, consulting, or whatever best describes the business<br>■ Description of product/service |
| Target market: | ■ For trading: buying from _____ and selling to _____<br>■ For service: location of service delivery and location of client |
| Personal experience: | ■ Description of personal experience and years of involvement in a similar business |
| Academic qualifications: | ■ University or above _____<br>■ Completed secondary _____<br>■ Others _____ |
| Reason for having bank account in Hong Kong: | ■ Describe relationship of the business with China/HK;<br>■ Purpose of bank account to receive money from China/HK<br>■ Purpose if used to pay a supplier in China/HK |
| Major way and frequency of using bank account and number of transactions per year: | ■ Money transactions mainly by wire transfer?<br>■ Require any L/C service?<br>■ Estimate of how many times money in and out each month and for the first 12 months |
| Expected income for 1st year: | ■ Estimation of income (not profit), mainly about the |

| | amount of money that will go through the bank account |
|---|---|
| Source of fund for the business (e.g., work, family business, etc.): | ■ Source of funds used for starting the business – from work, from family business, etc. |
| Counterparties (for which funds transfer through the account): | ■ Please give the main source of funds<br>■ _____% from _____ (country)<br>■ _____% from _____ (country)<br>■ Please give the main application of funds<br>■ _____% to _____ (country)<br>■ _____% to _____ (country) |

| | |
|---|---|
| Management office address: | ■ Regular address to manage the business<br>■ Can be located in any country<br>■ Can be a home office |
| Correspondence address: | ■ For receiving banking materials, such as online banking PIN, bank statement, etc.<br>■ Can use Hong |

|  | Kong registered address |
|---|---|
| Contact method with bank: | ■ Telephone:<br>■ Fax:<br>■ Mobile:<br>■ Email: |

**W**hy do you need a Hong Kong visa?
If you were not born in Hong Kong, you need a Hong Kong visa that allows to you work and live in Hong Kong.

**What types of visas are most common for business owners?**

1.     Employment/work visa

If you are an employee or if you want to work for a company in Hong Kong, you should get an employer to sponsor you to get a work/employment visa.

2. Entrepreneur/investment visa

If you are a business owner and would like to expand your business in Hong Kong or China, you can set up a limited company in Hong Kong and have it sponsor you to obtain an entrepreneur or investment visa.

3. Student visa

If you are admitted to study in one of the universities in Hong Kong, you can apply for a student visa, which allows you to work in Hong Kong for one year after you complete your degree.

**What is the benefit of getting a Hong Kong visa?**

After you get a work, entrepreneur, or student visa, you and your dependents can work, live, or study in Hong Kong without any restrictions. Dependents are defined as an opposite sex spouse (legally married) and children below age 18.

A spouse on a dependent visa is free to work or start a business in Hong Kong with no restrictions. Children can also apply to attend private schools.

The visas granted are subject to renewal upon expiration. After seven years of continuous residence in Hong Kong, you will get a permanent Hong Kong identity card. Then you can live in Hong Kong permanently or leave Hong Kong and come back when you choose to live there in the future.

Visas are usually granted on a two-year basis and are renewable for another two years in the pattern of 2+2+2+1. After the seven-year period, you will go through an interview with the Immigration Department to confirm you have already satisfied all the criteria and would be able to get a permanent Hong Kong identity card.

There is no absolute guarantee of success of getting a permanent Hong Kong identity card after the seven-year period of staying in Hong Kong. The immigration department reserves the final discretion of approval. However, in normal cases, if the applicants can show good employment and business records with no criminal offenses, the chance of approval is optimistic.

**Timeline for applying and getting approval for the visa**
The Immigration Department usually takes six to eight weeks to review the documents and process the case, assuming all documents are ready. However, they may come back to request additional information. To play safe, it is advised to allow three months for the whole process.

**What are the key success factors for an employment/work visa?**
To succeed, the following critical factors have to be present:
1. A real and valid employment offer from an established company.
2. Candidates must possess qualifications and working experience relevant to the post offer.
3. A job specification of the post should be one that

requires more knowledge, skills, and experience.

4. The salary level should be at least HK$30,000 per month. Of course, the higher the salary level, the better. This is to ensure that the expat staff will not compete directly with the local workforce for junior job openings.

5. Justification by the employer as to why the post cannot be filled locally.

6. The employing company has to be a financially sound company with an established business history. Although it does not need to prove it makes a high profit, it at least reports profits tax, employs local employees, maintains a physical office in Hong Kong, etc.

### What are the key success factors for an entrepreneur/investment visa?

To succeed in sponsoring the business owner to obtain an entrepreneur visa, the following factors are important:

1. The company needs to have some history in the industry. For example, it must show it has been in business for one to two years.

2. The company has a sound business model with an established client base.

3. Above all, and most importantly, the company benefits the Hong Kong society as a whole by creating local employment. Although there is no ratio of local employees to one expat, the Immigration Department usually looks upon it favorably when the

company has local full-time employees. The more local jobs created, the better.

4. Although there is no specific requirement for how much the entrepreneur needs to invest in the company in order to warrant the successful application of the entrepreneur/investment visa, I would suggest one should inject at least HK$200,000 (equivalent to USD25,000) in the company to show that the company has sufficient resources to kick off and develop the business. This amount of money has to be deposited into the bank account during the time of visa application. Thereafter, it does not need to be kept there, and you can apply the money for other purposes.

**Documents required for applying for the employment/work visa**

Employer

1. Business registration license
2. Certificate of incorporation
3. Article of association
4. Latest annual return
5. Latest profits tax return
6. Latest audited financial statements
7. A list of staff employed by the company with names, title, and salary
8. Office lease agreement
9. Company brochure (can download the

website)
10. Justification for the necessity of the post
11. Job description of the post
12. Why the job cannot be recruited locally
13. Last three months' bank statements showing transaction volume

Employee

1. CV of the candidate
2. School certifications
3. Reference letters from previous employers
4. Passport copies of the applicant and their dependents
5. Two passport-size photos of the application and each of the dependent

**Documents required for applying for the entrepreneur/investment visa**
1. Passport copies of the applicant and their dependents
2. Two passport-size photos of the applicant and their dependents
3. Sponsoring company's latest audited financial statements
4. Sponsoring company's setup documents showing the shareholders
5. Sponsoring company's latest three months of bank account statements showing transaction volume
6. CV of the shareholder or directors (supported by school certificates and previous employers'

reference letters, if any)
7. Business plan that includes the following:
   - Business activities
   - Financial forecast
   - Source of fund and paid capital
   - Customer profiles
   - Products/services description
   - Marketing strategies
   - Recruitment plan
8. Projects or sales orders or customers on hand, if any

## Why should you engage a professional firm to apply for a Hong Kong visa?

You can apply for a Hong Kong visa by downloading and filling in the forms from the immigration department. Here is the link:

https://www.immd.gov.hk/

However, I strongly recommend you get a professional firm to handle the application because there are a lot of hidden rules. A visa application is not simply about submitting forms and documents. It is about presenting your case strategically so that it fits into the development plan of Hong Kong and the agenda of the Hong Kong government. In other words, you need to show how your business will contribute to the success of the strategic plan of the Hong Kong government.

You are not obliged to use professional firms to

apply for the Hong Kong visa. However, professional firms know the rules and how to present your case in the best light that appeals to the Immigration Department.

You are welcome to contact me at eunicechuchu@gmail.com for a free consultation and initial assessment if you have any questions.

Good luck on your visa application!

T o run a business in Hong Kong, you need to be equipped with some very basic knowledge about the Hong Kong tax system. Any type of company in Hong Kong needs to handle two types of tax reporting:

    a. Employer's return
    b. Profits tax return

**Employer's return (Forms IR56A and IR56B)**
A company has to report to the Hong Kong government how much it has paid in salaries to **each** of its staff, including the director, in April every year. IR56A is the cover sheet that states how many staff are reported, and IR56B reports all the details of each of the staff employed during the year. These details are below:

    a. Staff name
    b. Address
    c. HK identity card number
    d. Marital status
    e. Position held
    f. Salaries, housing, and bonus paid during the period of April 1 to March 31 of the next year.

Failing to file these employer returns will result in a penalty. Even when a company employs no one, it has to file a "zero" return.

All the employer's returns have to be submitted on or before April 30 each year.

**Profits tax rates**
There are two tiers of profit tax rates:
1. Profits below HK$2 million are subject to 8.25%.
2. Profits above HK$2 million are subject to 16.5%.

When a person controls several companies, he or she can only nominate one company to take advantage of the 8.25% preferential tax rate, while all other companies would be subject to the 16.5% profits tax. Control is defined as owning over 50% of the shares.

In a group of companies with a parent and subsidiaries, only one company within the group can enjoy the 8.25% tax rate, while the rest of the companies have to pay a 16.5% profits tax.

If a couple owns three companies and each of them owns 50% of each of the three companies, then none of the three companies are controlled by either one of them. All three of these companies can enjoy the 8.25% rate.

If two friends or siblings own three companies and each of them owns 50% of each of the three companies, then none of the three companies are controlled by either of them. All three of these companies can enjoy the 8.25% profits tax rate.

## Financial year end

A limited company needs to set its own financial year end. In Hong Kong, companies can choose any date as their financial year end.

The fiscal year of the Hong Kong government is from April 1 to March 31 of the next year. Because of this, many companies choose for their financial year to also be from April 1 to March 31, which coincides with the fiscal year of the government. In such circumstances, their internal financial records of salaries paid to each staff can easily tally back to the numbers reported to the government.

Other limited companies prefer the calendar year to be from January 1 to December 31.

## Timing of reporting profits tax returns

For sole proprietorship and partnership:

For sole proprietors and partners in partnerships, the profits tax is reported in May every year when the profits tax returns are issued. The deadline of submission is three months from the issue of the profits tax return (i.e., July 31 each year).

For limited companies:

For a limited company, there are a number of dates to watch out for. When a company is first set up, the profits tax return will only be issued after 18 months from the date of incorporation. Then the company is given an additional three months to prepare and file the returns. However, 18 months is the maximum period; this does not mean you have to wait 18 months before you take action to prepare for the financial statements and tax filing.

For example, when a company is set up on January 1, Year 1, it can choose its year end to be one of the following:
A) December 31 of the same year – 12-month period
B) March 31 of the next year – 15-month period that coincides with the fiscal year end of the government
C) June 30 of the next year – 18-month period

The company can start to prepare the bookkeeping, auditing, and profits tax filing right after its chosen financial year end. By the time it gets to the profits tax return in June, Year 2 (18 months after the date of incorporation on January 1, Year 1), it can immediately fill in the details and submit the profits tax return to the Inland Revenue Department (IRD), together with the audited financial statements.

After the company files the first profits tax return 18 months from the date of incorporation, it falls into the regular tax filing cycle of reporting tax every 12 months from the financial year end of the company.

The normal profits tax filing deadline for all limited

companies is on April 30, which is 30 days after the issue of the profits tax return by the IRD on April 1 each year.

However, limited companies can apply for a profits tax filing extension in the following manner:

|  | Extended tax deadline |
|---|---|
| A. Limited companies with the year ending on December 31 (D code) | August 15 of the following year |
| B. Limited companies with the year ending on March 31 (M code | November 15 of the same year |
| C. Limited companies with the year ending on a date other than these two days | April 30 (No extension) |

### Statutory auditing
The financial statements of the sole proprietorship and partnership do not need to be audited. They are required to be certified true and correct by the sole proprietor or the partners.

However, the financial statements of limited companies are required to be audited each year by certified public accountants in Hong Kong.

When filing with the profits tax return to the Inland Revenue Department, the following are required to be submitted together:
1. The statutory audited financial statements of the company
2. Tax computation
3. The profits tax return (PTR)

## Bookkeeping and accounting
All companies, including sole proprietorships, partnerships, and limited companies, have to prepare bookkeeping, which forms the basis of profits tax filing.

According to the regulations of Hong Kong, these bookkeeping records have to be kept for at least seven years.

If the transaction volume of your company is not high, you may choose to use Excel to keep track of the records with three worksheets:
   a)    Invoices issued to customers: This should show the date of invoice, the invoice number, customers' names, the amount in foreign currency and Hong Kong dollar equivalent, and settlement dates that agree with the bank statements.
   b)   Expenses incurred: This should show the date of suppliers' invoices, the invoice number, suppliers' names, amount, and the settlement dates

that agree with the bank statements.

c) The bank movement: This should mirror the bank statements with the description of the receipts and payments.

For most companies, I strongly recommend you use simple accounting software that helps you organize everything. There is now online, cloud-based accounting software, such as Xero, that has the following great features:

1. No initial investment is required. You only need to subscribe to the service for a small fee (i.e., USD40 per month). You can stop at any time without a commitment.

2. You can issue sales invoices through Xero, which directly keeps track of the settlement status.

3. Xero is interfaced with bank accounts, such as HSBC, DBS, and Neat. Every time that you log into Xero, the bank in and bank out transactions are automatically interfaced in Xero. You only need to match the bank in with invoices and Xero will automatically update the accounts receivable, generating an outstanding list of invoices in real time.

4. You can scan the suppliers and expenses invoices, hotel bill, and airline tickets and email to your Xero inbox. This way, you do not need to keep piles of paper for years.

5. You can even assign your accountant to be the advisor of Xero, who will then take care

of the bookkeeping for you and produce the financial statements instantly.

6. Xero can be accessed through mobile phones, tablets, or laptops, which allows you to manage your company anywhere you go.

Please note that I am not promoting Xero. There are other software options available, such as Quick-Books and Peachtree, that offer similar functions. I just want to show you the tools you can use to manage and organize your business on a continuous basis. This would also allow you to produce the financial records readily for the statutory audit and/or submission to the IRD when they are due.

## What kind of business records should be kept?

All kinds of documents that record the business transactions have to be kept either in hard copies or electronically which can be retrieved when they are required. Here are some examples. This list is by no means exhaustive.

a. Sales invoices issued to customers.
b. Purchases invoices issued by suppliers.
c. Expenses invoices or receipts.
d. Debit notes or credits notes issued or received.
e. All bank statements, remittance advices, credit notes.
f. Rental agreements.
g. Contracts: Sales contracts, distribution con-

tracts, employment contracts, etc.

h. Audited financial statements.

i. Tax records such as tax assessments, tax returns, correspondence with the tax authority

## How long the business records have to be kept?

All the business records have to be kept for at least seven years. If there is no dispute between your company and the tax authority or customers or suppliers, the business records can be disposed after seven years. However, if there are any disputes, the business records have to be kept and retained properly until all the disputes are resolved.

Should you prefer a one-on-one discussion, please feel free to contact me at eunicechuchu@gmail.com.

# T erritorial tax system

Hong Kong follows a territorial tax system, which means only profits that are sourced from Hong Kong will be subject to Hong Kong profits tax. In other words, if the profits are sourced outside Hong Kong, they will not be subject to Hong Kong profits tax.

Whether a company is entitled to offshore profit treatment is a matter of fact. Typically, the Inland Revenue Department (IRD) would raise lots of questions around the company's method of organization and operation and require transactional paper trails to support the claim of offshore profit treatment. Such a fact-finding exercise can be quite extensive. Based on the patterns of fact as established, it will then be necessary to determine the sources of profits and the geographical location of the sources. There have been numerous tax cases that provide helpful principles, but the application of such principles in particular cases can still be highly controversial. Arguments entail detailed analysis of the fact patterns as well as technical analysis to find out the best position to take and strategy for pursuing the claim. The quality of evidence is most important, so the availability of transactional paper trails is a must.

## Is Hong Kong a tax haven?
The United Nation labeled a number of jurisdictions as being tax havens, and Hong Kong was once on the list, although it was ultimately removed. Tax haven refers to a place that charges no or low corporate tax and thus creates an opportunity for corporations to shift their profits to this tax haven despite no or little business operation actually taking place there.

## Changing the international tax landscape
In 2014 the Organisation of Economic Corporation and Development (OECD) issued principles and guidelines of Base Erosion and Profit Shifting (BEPS) to combat companies shifting their profits to low-tax countries and avoiding the profits tax that they are liable for where they are operating.

## Would the IRD grant offshore profit treatment?
With all of these changes in international tax laws, the Hong Kong IRD is now reluctant to grant offshore profits treatment easily. Theoretically, if the business operations that generate profits take place outside Hong Kong, the chance of getting this offshore profits treatment is still slim, if not impossible.

When a Hong Kong company maintains no office in Hong Kong, employs no staff in Hong Kong, all the directors and shareholders live outside Hong Kong, and the customers are based internationally, then the IRD will challenge the taxpayer on why they need a Hong Kong company.

If a Hong Kong company is sourcing its profits outside Hong Kong, then it must have sourced it somewhere else in the world. The logical question will then be, where and in which country are the company's profits taxed? If the answer is the company pays no corporate tax to any government on its profits at all, it seems that the company is taking part in tax evasion.

At the end of this chapter, I have attached a list of standard questions raised by the IRD when a company submits an offshore claim for your reference. It is by no means an official guideline. It only aims to provide readers a brief idea of what information the IRD is looking for and what type of transactional evidence is required. Further questions may be raised depending on particular cases.

### Recommendation
I usually explain to business owners that they need to pay some kind of corporate tax on their profits. They can only minimize the amount legally by utilizing all the eligible claims and allowances, but they should not attempt to avoid it completely. The purpose of running a profitable business is to provide a fulfilling life for the entrepreneur and a comfortable environment for their families. Why, then, create a risk that will cause the entrepreneur

and their family to worry for an indefinite period of time?

The Hong Kong profits tax rates are already very low compared to many countries in the world. I strongly recommend entrepreneurs comply with all the tax rules. If they want bigger profits after taxes, they should focus on improving their business performance rather than minimizing the tax liability illegally. Both require effort on the part of the business owners, yet the latter entails significant risk. If you have any questions, please feel free to contact me at eunicechuchu@gmail.com.

ΔΔΔ

*Appendix*

*Sample list of questions issued by IRD to companies applying for "offshore claim"*

<u>Business establishment</u>

*(1)    An organization chart and details of the company's establishments in Hong Kong and outside of Hong Kong. This should include the full address and size of the office, the number of employees and their respective names, post titles, duties, and remuneration packages.*

*(2)    For an establishment outside of Hong Kong, describe in detail its functions and specify its authorities if it was involved in negotiations with buyers and suppliers.*

*(3)        If there is no establishment outside of Hong Kong, provide details of the intermediary through which the offshore activities were affected and its general authorities.*

*(4)    Service agreement and minutes of directors' meetings for appointment of the intermediary mentioned in (3) above*

<u>Service income</u>
<u>The company's mode of operation</u>

*(5)    A detailed description of the functions carried out by the company in order to earn the service income. For each of the activities identified, specify the name of the responsible person and the place where such activity was performed. This analysis should in-*

clude the following:

  a. How the client was sourced
  b. How the service fee was negotiated
  c. How the service was provided

(6) In respect to the reported service income, provide detailed breakdowns of the sums received from each of the payers.

(7) For each payer mentioned in (6) above, provide the following:

  a. The name and address of the payer and its relationship with the company, its director, and its shareholder
  b. The nature of services rendered
  c. The basis of computing the service fee
  d. A copy of the service agreement

*Representative transaction*

(8)  For the largest amount of the service fee mentioned in (6) above, provide an analysis of each step of the significant activities carried out by the company in earning the income, the place(s) of the service, and the name and post title of the responsible person.

(9)  To demonstrate how the activities described in (8) above have been carried out by the company, provide a full indexed set of documents that includes the following:

a.  Correspondence, email, fax, or agreement with clients.

b.  A travel schedule of each of the responsible persons,

*showing (for each trip) the date of departure from/ arrival to Hong Kong, the place and purpose of each visit, and the period of stay with copies of their traveling documents.*

c. *The invoice and debit notes issued by the company to the service fee payer in respect to the services rendered.*

d. *A computation showing how the service fee was calculated and the banking documents.*

a. *Correspondence, email, or agreement with clients.*

b. *A travel schedule of each of the responsible persons, showing (for each trip) the date of departure from/arrival to Hong Kong, the place and purpose of each visit, and the period of stay with copies of their traveling documents.*

c. *The invoice and debit notes issued by the company to the service fee payer in respect to the services rendered.*

d. *A computation showing how the service fee was calculated and the banking documents.*

## *Trading income*
### *The company's products*

*(10) The type of goods being purchased are sold with a copy of the catalog number or price list/quotation of the products issued by the company in the relevant basis period*

*The company's mode of trading*

(11) *Full details on how the company carried out the claimed offshore trading transactions, including the following:*

a. *Whether the sales were on an indent basis or inventories were held for filling up orders, and in the latter case, advise the place where the inventory was kept*

b. *Whether samples were produced to potential customers, and if yes, provide full details of how, where, and by whom the samples were produced and delivered to the customers*

c. *Whether the company's own sales staff was sent overseas to negotiate and conclude sales and, if yes, a full list of all staff involved in the claimed offshore operations; their names; Hong Kong Identity Card number; post title; and a full set of itinerary of the business trips made during the relevant basis period, including the period of each trip, the places visited, the purposes of each visit, and the suppliers/customers contacted*

d. *Whether overseas group companies or any other parties were involved in the offshore transactions and, if yes, the staff employed by each of these overseas companies; their respective names; Hong Kong Identity Card numbers; post titles; and a full set of itineraries of the business trips made, including the period of each trip, the place visited, the purpose of each visit, and the supplier/cus-*

tomers contacted

### The company's purchases

*(12)* *For the year of assessment involved, provide an analysis of the suppliers, giving their respective names, addresses, amount of yearly purchases and relationship with the company, and its directors or shareholders, if any. If the number of suppliers exceeds 15, provide a list of the 10 largest suppliers with the above details.*

*(13)* *Provide full details of how, where, and by whom the suppliers were procured and how the purchase price of the goods was determined. If by negotiation, explain how, where, and by whom the negotiations were carried out. If there was a long-established business relationship, provide full details of how this relationship was established. If the suppliers were group companies, confirm whether the products supplied and the purchase prices were predetermined according to group policy or if the company had the authority to determine the purchase prices and/or adjust the prices such as by way of discount.*

*(14)* *Confirm whether any distribution agreement or other form of master agreement was entered into with any of the suppliers and, if yes, provide a copy.*

*(15)* *For individual transactions, confirm whether a formal purchase contract was made for every order/repeated order. Describe how, where, and by whom the contract was prepared and signed.*

*(16)* *Provide full details of how, where, and by whom*

the purchase order was initiated, processed, and placed with the supplier and whether confirmation from the supplier is required.

(17) Provide full details of the method of financing the purchase of goods and how payment was made to the suppliers. In respect to banking facilities obtained by the company to finance the purchases, provide a copy of the banking facility letter of the relevant period showing the extent of the facility obtained and the security provided. Advise the names of staff authorized by the company to act as signatories of the company's bank accounts.

### The company's sales

(18) For the year of assessment involved, provide an analysis of the customers, giving their respective names, addresses, amount of yearly sales and relationship with the company, and its directors or shareholders, if any. If the number of customers exceeds 15, provide a list of the 10 largest customers with the above details.

(19) Provide full details of how, where, and by whom the customers were solicited and how the selling price of the goods was determined. If by negotiation, explain how, where, and by whom the negotiations were carried out. If there was a long-established business relationship, provide full details of how this relationship was established. If the customers were group companies, confirm whether the products sold and the selling prices were predetermined according to group policy or if the company had the authority to determine the

*selling prices and/or adjust the prices such as by way of discount.*

*(20)Whether any distribution agreement or master sale agreement was entered into with any of the customers and, if yes, provide a copy*

*(21) For individual transactions, confirm whether a formal sales contract was made for every order/repeated order. Explain how, where, and by whom the contract was prepared and signed.*

*(22) Full details of how, where, and by whom the purchase order from the customer was initiated, processed, and placed with the company; the name of staff who had the ultimate authority to accept the order; and whether confirmation with the customer was required*

*(23) Full details of how, where, and by whom the shipment of goods from suppliers to customers was arranged and the inspection of goods before shipment was made, whether the goods from suppliers passed through Hong Kong or not, and if the goods passed through Hong Kong, whether transshipment was instantly arranged or whether they were temporarily stored in the company's warehouse*

*(24) Advise how customers settled their accounts (e.g., by letter of credit, bill of exchange, etc.).*

*Representative transactions*

(25) For the two largest sales transactions in terms of sales value with the largest customer, provide a full indexed set of documents in chronological order, including sales and purchase agreements, purchase and sales orders, order confirmation, correspondence by way of letters, facsimile transmissions, emails, invoices, letter of credit, shipping and insurance documents, etc.

(26) For the two transactions selected above:

a. Details of the nature, quantity, and value of the products purchased and sold as well as the parties involved

b. Clear and full version of each document with a brief description of the nature of the document and the parties concerned

c. The routing of documents (i.e., the sender and recipient of the documents). By reference to the documents, describe thoroughly how, where, and by whom the purchase and sales activities were performed from negotiations with buyers and suppliers, conclusion of contracts, issue and receipt of sales and purchase orders, confirmation and acceptance of the orders, arrangement of finance, inspection, and delivery of goods to final settlement of accounts.

## Basis of the offshore claim

(27) Give the reasons why the claimed offshore profits

*are not chargeable to Hong Kong Profits Tax.*

*(28) Confirm if any of the company's profits have been subject to tax in any jurisdiction, and provide relevant tax documents if the answer is in the affirmative.*

*Please reply within one month from the date of this letter.*

**S**alaries from sole proprietorships and partnerships

When the sole proprietorships and partnerships are making a profit, their business owners can withdraw money as salaries to support themselves and their families. The amount they should withdraw every month as a salary will depend on the profits of the sole proprietorships and partnerships. If the sole proprietorships and partnerships are making very good profits, their business owners can withdraw whatever amount they like. If the sole proprietorships and partnerships are not making good profits, I suggest not withdrawing excessive salaries. Otherwise, they will need to inject capital to meet the operation needs of the sole proprietorships or partnerships in the future.

As sole proprietorships and partnerships are not legal entities that are independent of their business owners, the profits generated are all accrued to the owners. Hence, whatever salaries are withdrawn by the business owners from the sole proprietorships and partnerships are not tax deductible.

In other words, it does not matter how much of a salary the business owners withdraw from the sole proprietorships and partnerships. The amount withdrawn will be disregarded when calculating the profits tax liability of these entities.

For example, when the sole proprietorships/partnerships make $100 in surplus, the business owners withdraw $60 as salaries, leaving $40 as the profits. But when calculating tax, the IRD still takes $100 as the profits and subjects it to profits tax. The $40 in salary pay to the sole proprietor or partners is disregarded as expenses.

### Salaries from limited companies

For the rest of this chapter, I will focus on limited companies, as this is the most common form of business operation.

Please note that only directors can get salaries or a director fee from the companies, not the shareholders. Shareholders can only get dividends at the end of the year when the directors propose to pay a dividend from the retained earnings of the company. In other words, shareholders may or may not get any dividends every year. Hence, if you want to get a monthly salary from the profits of the company, you should make yourself the director.

When the director is not a shareholder at the same time, it means that he or she is only a senior employee in the company. Therefore, the salary or bonuses he or she will receive will be stipulated in the employment contract, and the company has to honor the terms of the employment contract accordingly. The amount of the salary or bonuses of these senior employees would be paid in accordance with the employment contracts.

However, when the director is also a shareholder (business owner) of the company, should he or she get a monthly salary when the limited company is making a profit?

### Should the business owner get a monthly salary from the company?

This question needs to be answered from two perspectives: One is from the cash flow perspective, and the other is from the tax reporting perspectives.

### Cash flow perspective

When the limited company is making a profit, then the directors, who are also the shareholders, should definitely withdraw money to support their own living expenses. However, this should be done in a disciplined way.

The directors at a limited company should calculate the minimum amount they need to support themselves and their families on a monthly basis and arrange a "salary payment" of this amount to be transferred from the company's bank account to their own personal bank account. The excess profits will be retained in the company for future operating use. By the end of the year, if the company is really doing great and has accumulated good profits, then the directors/shareholders can arrange a bigger bonus (not a dividend) to reward themselves. This way they can avoid draining the cash flow of the company when excessive salaries are paid out and subsequently needing to inject capital into the company again to meet the operational needs. This is particularly important to avoid disputes when there are several shareholders in the company.

If the company is not making any profits or the cash inflows from customers are just enough to cover the operation expenses, then the directors, who are the shareholders at the same time, should refrain from receiving any salaries from the company to avoid a further cash flow drain of the company.

**Tax reporting perspective**

First of all, when reporting salaries paid by a company to its directors, the period covered will be from April 1 to March 31, as this needs to match with the fiscal year of the Hong Kong government.

When reporting the amount of salaries a director, who is the shareholder at the same time, gets from the company during a particular year, this amount does not necessarily tie to or agree with the amount of actual cash outflow. In other words, the amount of cash a director actually withdraws can be higher or lower than the amount that is reported to the IRD. The purpose is to achieve maximum tax efficiency.

The amount to be reported to the IRD should utilize all of the allowances entitled to the directors. In Hong Kong, each person enjoys a personal allowance that is tax free. Currently the personal allowance amount is HK$132,000 per year. When a director gets HK$132,000 as a salary, he or she pays zero salaries tax, while the company can have a HK$132,000 salaries expense to drive down the profit.

When the director is married and his or her spouse is not working, then he or she gets another HK$132,000 married person allowance. If he or she has two children, he or she can get a HK$100,000 allowance per child. Hence the total allowance the director enjoys will be HK$464,000. If the limited company reports paying a salary of HK$464,000 to the director, he or she personally still does not need to pay any salaries tax. Meanwhile, the limited company would have HK$464,000 in salary expenses to drive down their profits.

For example, if the company makes a profit of HK$1 million, without declaring any salary paid to the director, it has to pay a profits tax of HK$82,500. By declaring paying salaries of HK$464,000 to the director, the company only needs to pay a profits tax of HK$44,220 [8.25% x ($1m - $464,000)], while the director does not need to pay any salaries tax. Overall, there is a tax savings of HK$38,280, or 46%.

## Salaries tax

So far, we have assumed the director does not pay any salaries tax. But in fact, he or she should pay a small salaries tax of HK$4,000 to maximize the overall tax benefits.

Any salaries earned by the director, after deducting for the allowance he or she is entitled to, will be subject to a salaries tax. However, the first two HK$50,000 blocks are subject to lower tax rates, as follows:

| | Subject to | Below 8.25% profits tax rate Amount of salaries tax |
|---|---|---|
| First HK$50,000 | 2% | HK$1,000 |
| Second HK$50,000 | 6% | HK$3,000 |
| Third HK$50,000 | 10% | HK$5,000 |
| Fourth HK$50,000 | 14% | HK$7,000 |
| Balance | 17% | |

Below 8.25% profits tax rate

The first HK$50,000 is subject to 2% only, and the second HK$50,000 is subject to 6% only, which are lower than the corporate profits tax rate of 8.25%.

As a result, if the director gets a salary of HK$564,000 ($464,000 allowance + $100,000 salaries that are subject to lower salaries tax rates), he or she only needs to pay HK$4,000, whereas the company would have $564,000 salaries expense to drive down the profits to $436,000 ($1,000,000 profits - $564,000 salaries) and only needs to pay a profits tax of HK$35,970. Overall, the tax liabilities would be HK$39,970 ($35,970 + $4,000), which is lower than the original profits tax of HK$82,500 (HK$1,000,000 x 8.25%) by HK$42,530, or 52%.

When the limited company is making profits of HK $1 million, the total amount of tax payable is HK $39,970. So, the effective tax rate is only 3.99%.

I will suggest you consult your accountant on how much salary to report to the government that can best utilize your allowance and achieve the greatest overall tax benefits.

You are also welcome to contact me at eunicechuchu@gmail.com if you have any questions.

### The difference between salaries reported and cash withdrawals

As mentioned earlier, the amount of the cash withdrawal by the director, who is also a shareholder of the company, may be different from the amount of salaries tax reported to the government. The reasons for this are below:

1. Cash withdrawal is calculated to cover the costs of living of the director/shareholder and his or her family.
2. Salaries reported to the government are

calculated to utilize the amount of allowance the director is entitled to.

Therefore, there will be overpayment or underpayment. The difference will be treated as the amount due from (receivable from) the director or the amount due to (payable to) the director.

To continue with the above example, the director should report HK$564,000 as salaries to the government. Every month, the director withdraws HK$50,000 as his or her own salary. On an annual basis, he or she withdraws HK$600,000. The director over-withdraws HK$36,000 (HK$600,000 - HK$564,000), which will be treated as receivable from the director in the books of the company. Theoretically, the director has to refund this amount to the company when the company presents the debts and demands settlement. But, given that he or she is the business owner, the shareholder, and the director all at the same time, the only person who can act on behalf of the company to demand settlement is the business owner, shareholder, or director. Assuming there is no other shareholder or director in the company, he or she actually can leave this amount there forever until the company liquidates.

Alternatively, the director can also clear out this amount by declaring a dividend to him- or herself. The company has profits after tax of HK$400,030 (HK$436,000 profits less HK$35,970 profits tax). By right, he or she can declare all these profits after tax of HK$400,030 as dividends to him- or herself. But when withdrawing cash out as a dividend, he or she should only take cash of HK$364,030 because HK$36,000 is still owed to the company.

Normally, no director or shareholder will declare such a high dividend because sufficient funds need to be retained in the company to meet its operational needs. So, the director should balance the amount of cash he or she needs to retain in the company versus the amount he or she wants to take out from the business.

The director can simply declare a dividend of HK$136,000 as a dividend. After setting aside the amount that has to be refunded to the company, HK$36,000, he or she can take out cash of HK$100,000.


**Should the director/shareholder get a salary when the company is losing money?**
Whether the director/shareholder should get a salary from his or her own company when it is losing money would depend on whether he or she wants to borrow from banks or investors.
a)   If he or she does want to borrow from banks or investors, then he or she should not get any salary to avoid creating an even bigger loss and making the company less appealing to banks or potential investors.
b)   If he or she does not want to borrow from banks or investors, then he or she should at least

get a salary equal to the tax allowance he or she is entitled so that he or she does not need to pay any salaries tax on the one hand and the company has more expenses to enlarge the tax loss on the other. The tax loss can be carried forward to future years indefinitely to offset future profits and thereby reduce future profits tax.

For example, a company has a loss of HK$10,000. If it pays HK$132,000 as the director's salary, then its loss will be HK$142,000. In the next year, if the company makes a profit of HK$142,000, it still does not need to pay any profits tax.

I suggest you consult your accountant on how much salary to report to the government that utilizes your allowances and how much in dividends to pay out that can satisfy your personal cash needs, on one hand, and keep sufficient capital in the company for its operational needs.

You are also welcome to reach out to me at eunicechuchu@gmail.com if you want to discuss this further.

I t is very common for a sole proprietor in a sole proprietorship, partners in a partnership, or a director/shareholder in a limited company to pay expenses on behalf of the company. They are collectively referred to as business owners.

For example, the business owners may book airline tickets and hotel accommodations for a business trip using their own credit cards. Or they may buy lunches when they meet clients. All of these expenses are incurred on behalf of the company. How do you handle these expenses?

The simplest way is to claim these expenses from the company once a month. At each month's end, a business owner can file a summary of the costs he or she has incurred on behalf of the company. In this way, these expenses will be reflected as the costs of operation in the financial statements of the company.

Whether they get reimbursed from the company would depend on the cash flow status of the company. If the company has good cash flow, the company can make out a check to clear out the amount due to the business owners. However, if the company does not have sufficient cash flow, it can leave these amounts in the book until it has sufficient cash flow to pay back the business owners.

## What types of expenses can be claimed from the company?

All kinds of expenses that have to be incurred for the production of the assessable profits can be claimed by the company and become tax deductible. In other words, if those expenses are for the personal expenditures of the business owners, they should not be claimed by the company, as they would not be tax deductible in any way.

Some business owners put their household expenditures into the company. These would actually be removed in tax computation, so there is no tax benefit to include these expenditures into the company in the first place. I suggest that you only include legitimate business expenditures for the company.

Here are some of the legitimate expenditures for your consideration. This list is by no means exhaustive:

a. Office rental – If you are using your home as your office, then the portion of the rental used for business purposes can be charged to the company.

b. Insurance of the company – Personal insurance plans that have savings features will definitely not be allowed as tax-deductible expenses. Only charge simple insurance premiums to the company.

c. Salaries/Mandatory Provident Fund of staff and directors – If these are incurred for business purposes, they can be claimed as legitimate business expenditures.

d. Business trips – Airline tickets, accommodations, and local or overseas travel, as long as they are incurred for business purposes, can be charged to the company

e. Depreciation of equipment and furniture/ leasehold improvements

f. Computer, Internet services, printing, paper, courier charges, staff benefits, accounting fees, audit fees, company secretary fees, legal fees, advertising, office suppliers, bank charges, loan interests, entertainment for legitimate business purposes, utilities, etc.

## Appendix

*You can draw up a simple income statement that summarizes all incomes and expenditures. Then you will have a better view of the performance of your business.*

| Income statement | | $ |
|---|---|---|
| Revenue - sales of goods | | 1,000 |
| Revenue - service income | | 200 |
| Revenue - interest income | | 30 |
| Total revenue | A | 1,230 |
| | | |
| Expenditures | | |
| Rental of office / quarter | | 300 |
| Staff salaries | | 400 |
| Staff MPF | | 20 |
| Staff benefits | | 10 |
| Insurance | | 3 |
| Business trips | | 50 |
| Depreciation | | 40 |
| Computers / internet / mobile | | 30 |
| Printing / stationeries | | 10 |
| Accounting / auditing | | 20 |
| Legal / company secretary fee | | 10 |
| Advertising / promotion | | 60 |
| Entertainment | | 170 |
| Utilities | | 20 |
| Bank charges / loan interest | | 10 |
| Total expenditures | B | 1,153 |
| Profit before tax | A - B | 77 |
| Tax - 8.25% | | (6) |
| Profit after tax | | 71 |

# Eunice Chu

**Balance sheet**

|  |  | $ |
|---|---|---|
| **Assets** | | |
| Property, plant and equipment | | 600 |
| Bank balance | | 300 |
| Cash balances | | 20 |
| Accounts receivables | | 190 |
| Inventories | | 320 |
| Total assets | A | 1,430 |
| | | |
| **Liabilities** | | |
| Account payables | | (280) |
| Bank loans | | (560) |
| Tax payable | | (6) |
| Accruals | | (30) |
| Total liabilities | B | (876) |
| | | |
| Net asset value | A - B | 554 |
| | | |
| **Equity** | | |
| Share capital | | 200 |
| Retained earnings | | |
|   - prior year profits | | 283 |
|   - Current year profit | | 71 |
| Total shareholders' fund | A - B | 554 |

W hen the company expands its operations, it may need to employ local staff. There are a couple of steps to pay attention to.

## 1. Recruiting staff

When you put up a recruitment advertisement on recruitment websites or in newspapers, avoid mentioning the following, as it constitutes discrimination:

A. Age

B. Sex

C. Ethnicity

You should simply state the job description, the educational and experience requirements, and the contact details. It is up to you whether to disclose salaries or remuneration offered. Showing the salary offer will screen out those non-targeted candidates, but it may also limit the number of applications you eventually receive.

You can always hire recruitment agents to do the work by paying an agency fee.

## 2. Employment contract

When your company employs a staff member, you should arrange to sign a formal employment contract with him or her that lays out the employment terms. This serves to protect both you and the employee when there are disputes in the future.

For the terms of the employment contract, you have to at least comply with the Labour Ordinance of Hong Kong. You can offer them better terms than those stipulated in the Labour Ordinance, but the terms cannot be worse. Here are some of the basic terms you will need to know:

A. Minimum wage of HK$37.5 per hour
B. Annual leave: Seven working days per year with full salary payment
C. Termination: Either parties can provide notice of termination to the other parties to terminate the employment relationship in the following manner:
1. Terminate immediately within seven days of employment without extra compensation. For example, if they work for five days, you have to pay five days of salary and no extra compensation.
2. Terminate within the probation period (usually the first three months): Give seven day of notice. This means if you ask them to leave the company after they have completed the seven days of employment but within the probation period, say, on the tenth day, you have to

allow them to work an additional seven days for you from the date when you ask them to leave and pay up to their last date of employment (total of 17 days salary) or let them go immediately but still pay an extra seven days' salary as compensation in lieu of notice (total of 17 days salary).

3. Terminate after the probation period: Give one month of notice. For example, if you terminate them on June 1, you have to allow them to work until June 30 and pay them up to June 30. If you want them to disappear immediately, you still need to pay them up to June 30 as payment in lieu of notice.

D. Maternity leave: A permanent staff who has been employed under a continuous contract for not less than 40 weeks is entitled to maternity leave in the following manner:

1. Women: 14 weeks with salaries to be paid at 80% of the normal level

2. Men: Five working days with salaries to be paid at 80% of the normal level

## Mandatory Provident Fund (MPF) Schemes for permanent staff

According to the Mandatory Provident Fund Schemes Ordinance (Cap485), a company is obliged to contribute MPF for the staff they employ between the ages of 18 to 64 when it employs them continuously for 60 days. The amount will be contributed to a fund separately managed from the company, and it cannot be withdrawn until the staff reaches the age of 65, becomes disabled permanently, or leaves Hong Kong permanently after a formal declaration.

First, the company needs to create an MPF account with one of the services providers, such as AIA, Manulife, HSBC, or Bank of China, just to name a few.

The company is obligated to withhold 5% of the salaries of the employees (employee's contribution) and then match another 5% (employer's contribution). The total amount is required to be deposited into the MPF account of the company created with one of the MPF service providers mentioned above within ten days after each month end.

For example, you employ a marketing staff at a monthly salary of HK$10,000. At the month's end, you only pay HK$9,500 to the staff and withhold HK$500 (employee's contribution). Then you match another HK$500 (employer's contribution). The total amount of HK$1,000 (HK$500 x 2) will be contributed to the MPF account of the company within ten days after each month's end.

There is a cap of a 5% contribution at HK$1,500. In other words, the maximum amount that the employee and employer could contribute would be HK

$1,500 per party and thus HK$3,000 for both parties.

For example, you employ a marketing director at a monthly salary of HK$50,000. At each month end, you only pay HK$48,500 to the staff and withhold HK$1,500 (instead of 5% x HK$50,000 = HK$2,500) and match another HK$1,500 (employer's contribution). The total amount of HK$3,000 (HK$1,500 x 2) will be contributed to the MPF account of the company within ten days after each month's end.

Please note that a late contribution after the tenth day would lead to a 5% penalty on the amount due.

Employees with a monthly salary below HK$7,100 do not need to contribute MPF as an employee. However, the employer still needs to contribute the 5% for them. In other words, the employer will pay the full HK$7,100 to the employee, but he or she needs to pay the employer's contribution of HK$355 to the MPF account within ten day after each month's end.

### Mandatory Provident Fund (MPF) Scheme for casual workers
If a company employs casual or part-time workers, does it need to contribute MPF for those workers? The answer is still yes if you continuously employ them for 60 days.

I suggest you seek professional advice, as employee relationships have to be handled carefully to avoid labor disputes.

## MPF for a sole proprietor, partners, or directors who are also shareholders

How should you handle the MPF for a sole proprietor in a sole proprietorship, partners in a partnership, or directors who are also the shareholders of a limited company? We will refer to them collectively as "business owners."

Theoretically, the MPF rules that apply to staff would also apply to the business owners in the same manner. There is no difference at all.

But as business owners, they can determine how their salaries are to be paid. Instead of paying themselves monthly, which will lead to MPF liabilities, many of them simply choose not to pay themselves any salaries for 11 months and only pay themselves a huge salary/bonus of HK$564,000 in the twelfth month (HK$564,000 is a salary level that utilizes all the allowances and enjoys all low tax blankets for a family of four). This way, they only need to contribute MPF for one month. Remember, both the employee's and employer's contributions are capped at HK$1,500 each. Hence, even though they get huge salaries in the twelfth month, the maximum amount of MPF both the employee and employer contribute is HK$3,000 (HK$1,500 x 2 parties).

## How can business owners live without salaries for 11 months?

Remember, the cash withdrawals by the business owners every month are independent of the salary payment. Just because they do not get monthly salaries does not mean that they do not get a cash withdrawal from the company. Every month, the business owners can withdraw a standard amount (say HK$50,000) to cover their own living expenses. This cash withdrawal is treated as borrowing from the company instead of as a salary. This is because when the company's business operations require capital, the business owners may contribute money back into the company and "repay" the amount they borrowed.

So, although a business owner withdraws and borrows HK$50,000 each month and thus HK$600,000 per year, they only get a salary payment of HK$564,000 once a year in the twelfth month and contribute MPF of HK$3,000 once a year. The difference of HK$36,000 ($600,000 - $564,000) is treated as the amount borrowed by the business owner from the company.

Local staff recruitment and payroll can be taxing exercises. You can contact me at eunicechuchu@gmail.com for a free chat.

# CHAPTER 9: GOVERNMENT FUNDING FOR SMALL AND MEDIUM ENTERPRISES

To help small and medium enterprises (SMEs), the Hong Kong government offers a number of loans to be applied for by SMEs. The three most common loans are below and can be applied for by most of these businesses.

| Schemes | Objectives | Recipients |
|---|---|---|
| SME Loan Guarantee Scheme (SGS) by Trade and Industry Department | For acquiring (a) business installations and equipment or (b) meeting working capital requirements<br><br>Loan up to HK$12M with government guarantee up to HK$6M (50%) at prevailing market rates<br><br>Repayable within 5 years (maximum) | SMEs |
| Microfinance Scheme | For startup businesses, self-employed, or training, upgrading of skills or obtaining professional certification<br><br>8% to 9% interest rate<br><br>Repayable within 5 years | HKID card holders over 18 years old<br><br>HK$300,000 |
| SME Financing Guarantee Scheme (by HKMC Insurance Ltd) | Help SMEs and non-listed enterprises for meeting working capital and business needs. It can be a term loan or revolving loan<br><br>Maximum loan: HK$15M<br><br>Maximum repayment period: 7 years<br><br>At market prevailing rate | HK companies |

Apart from loans, the government also offers a number of grants that do not need to be repaid.

# Here are a number of them for your easy reference.

| Funding Schemes | Objectives | Recipients | Amount |
|---|---|---|---|
| SME Export Marketing Fund (EMF) | For SMEs to expand markets outside HK<br><br>When the entity spends $100, it can claim reimbursement from the government after the completion of the overseas promotion event. | SMEs | Actual reimbursement basis |
| Branding, Upgrading, Domestic sales (BUD) | For developing brands, upgrading operations and promoting sales in Mainland/ASEAN | HK companies | HK$1,000,000 |
| Technology Voucher Program | Support SMEs using technological services and solutions to improve productivity or to upgrade or transform their business processes.<br><br>Funding up to $400,000 for each eligible entity will be provided on a 2:1 matching basis.<br><br>The government will reimburse 2/3 of the total project costs, with a cap at HK$400,000. | HK companies | HK$400,000 |

For further details, eligibility, and the application procedure, you are welcome to contact me at eunicechuchu@gmail.com.

**W**hen a business owner wants to close down a company, there are several ways to go about doing this.

### Sole proprietorships or partnerships

To close down a sole proprietorship or partnership, you only need to inform the Inland Revenue Department (IRD) by filing form IRC3113 Notification of Cessation of Business.

https://www.ird.gov.hk/eng/paf/for.htm

### Limited companies

To close down a limited company, you can choose to either go through the de-registration process or liquidation.

### Deregistration

When the company has no debts (is solvent) and all the shareholders agree to close down the business, the easiest and simplest way is to deregister the company in the follow manner.

1. Submit an application to the IRD to get a "No Objection for De-registration" (NOD). The IRD will issue this letter only when it

is satisfied that you have submitted all the audited financial statements up to date and have fully paid all profits tax due.

2. After getting this NOD, the limited company can file the application of deregistration with the Companies Registry (CR) together with the NOD, plus pay a fee.

3. The CR will publish the notice of deregulation of the company in the Gazette. If no one objects to it after three months, the company will be deregistered. The whole process will take six to nine months.

Once the company is de-registered, all the money in the bank account will be frozen and surrendered to the government. Therefore, I strongly recommend the directors either close the bank account or withdraw all the money before commencing the deregistration process.

**Liquidation**
This is a more complicated process. When the company is insolvent and it owes debts that it is unable to settle, it can wait for the creditors to initiate a creditor involuntary liquidation. The process will be as follows:

1. The creditor who forces the liquidation of the company would submit to court the application for an involuntary liquidation.

2. A liquidator will be appointed to take control of the company

3. The liquidator will sell all the assets of the

company at the highest prices possible.

4. The proceeds will then be distributed in the following sequence:

a) Liquidator
b) Preferential creditors—staff and government debts
c) Secured creditors
d) Unsecured creditors on a prorated basis
e) Shareholders on a prorated basis

I would suggest you consult a professional accounting firm to handle the deregistration and liquidation process, as there are many steps and documents involved.

You are also welcome to contact me at eunicechuchu@gmail.com for further information and advice.

## Do Great Business in Hong Kong

Before you put this book on the shelf, please connect with me on social media. Drop me a note. I would like to hear about your business plan and progress.

If you have difficulties in your business, drop me an email at eunicechuchu@gmail.com. Even if I cannot help, I have connections and friends that may provide you with solutions and advice.

Once again, I wish you luck in your business venture!

www.ingramcontent.com/pod-product-compliance
Lightning Source LLC
Chambersburg PA
CBHW020604220526
45463CB00006B/2441